# The Ordinal

## and

# Its Revision

by

**Peter Toon**

*Librarian of Latimer House, Oxford*

SBN 901710 53 9

**GROVE BOOKS**

**BRAMCOTE     NOTTS.**

# CONTENTS

*First Impression* July 1974

SBN 901710 53 9

# PREFACE

Rites of Ordination were never a vital interest of mine until 1973 when I was ordained deacon in Walton Parish Church, Liverpool, at the age of thirty-four. To my surprise I found that the Rite used was a combination of Series 2 Holy Communion, the Anglican-Methodist Ordinal (1968) and the Ordinal of 1662. The only parts of the latter which were used were the two imperative formulae which begin: 'Take thou authority . . .' These took the place of the Prayer of Ordination from the Anglican-Methodist Rite (see Section 4 below). I believe that the reason for this insertion was to ensure the legality of the ordinations. The experience of this service (when I was a lecturer in theology in a College of Education), my subsequent appointment to the staff of Latimer House, and my joining the Liturgy Group served to encourage me to study rites of ordination. What follows is part of the result of that brief study. I wish to record my thanks to my colleague, Roger T. Beckwith and to members of the Liturgy Group for their help.

After I had completed the manuscript of this booklet the ACCM Report on the Diaconate appeared, as did also the book by E. Echlin entitled, *The Story of Anglican Ministry.* Also, after the completion of the writing, I was ordained priest in Liverpool Cathedral. The contents of the service of ordination were so extraordinary that I have, at the proof stage, added an Appendix listing them. I feel justified in listing them and making a few comments because, when I saw the order of service, I fervently requested of the Cathedral staff that they restore the service to a closer relation with the Ordinal of 1662. My request was refused. I do now hope and pray that, until Synod approves the trial use of a new Ordinal, the diocese of Liverpool *(whose Bishops I highly esteem in the Lord)* will continue to use that of 1662. It is not only respect for law and order which prompts me to write this. Another concern is ecumenical. How can members of commissions of the Church of England discuss reunion and the validity of Anglican rites and orders when they cannot guarantee to Roman, Orthodox, Presbyterian or other non-episcopal bodies that the dioceses of the Church of England (or the chapters of Cathedrals) use the appointed rites of the Church?

Peter Toon

14 July, 1974

# 1. INTRODUCTION

In the Reformation of the sixteenth century when the Continental and Scottish Churches abandoned the historic threefold ministry of bishops, priests and deacons, the English Church decided to preserve it. Reformers such as John Calvin, John Knox and Theodore Beza argued that in the New Testament presbyters (priests) and bishops are two titles for one and the same minister of Christ; the elevation of the bishop as an officer above the presbyter was an innovation and one of the marks of the 'progress of corruption' in the Church. For these men the authority of the New Testament was decisive not only in matters of faith and morals but also in Church government. So they equated the offices of presbyter and bishop to make one order of the ministry. To assist such ministers they appointed laymen as deacons and as ruling-elders.[1] The English Reformers, however, while accepting that in the New Testament period the terms 'presbyter' and 'bishop' were probably two titles for one and the same minister, argued that there were stronger reasons for reforming rather than abolishing the historic, threefold ministry.[2] Therefore this ministry, cleansed of many of its medieval accretions, was preserved and has continued in the Church of England and in Anglican Churches to this day.

There were many people in the sixteenth century, and there have been many since, who have believed and argued that the origin of the threefold ministry is to be traced to the apostolic age and that it was actually inaugurated by the apostles. Such an interpretation has been placed on the words of the Preface to the Ordinal of the Book of Common Prayer (1662) which read: 'it is evident unto all men diligently reading Holy Scripture and ancient authors that from the apostles' time there have been three orders of ministers in Christ's Church: Bishops, Priests and Deacons'. This notion is of course a mistaken one. The ministry in local churches in the first century, as may be seen from the evidence in the New Testament, the Didache, the First Letter of Clement of Rome and the Letters of Ignatius of Antioch, was varied not uniform.[3] It was only gradually that the differentiation of bishop from presbyter emerged and it was the challenge of Montanism in the mid-second century (with its 'inspired' teachers and preachers) that hastened the process of the establishment of the threefold ministry in all places. The doctrine of apostolic succession (in terms of the succession of bishops in given sees since the time of the apostles) also came into prominence at this time. Later, that is in the third century and afterwards, Christians believed that there had always been a threefold ministry.

---

[1] See further J. L. Ainslie, *The Doctrines of Ministerial Order in the Reformed Churches*, 1940.

[2] Cf. *English Reformers* (Lib. of Christian Classics, Vol. XXVI), ed. T. H. L. Parker, 1966, pp.21ff and 39ff.

[3] For details see L. Goppelt, *Apostolic and Post-Apostolic Times*, trans. R. A. Guelich, 1970, and H. von Campenhausen, *Ecclesiastical Authority and Spiritual Power in the Church*, trans. J. A. Baker, 1969. Cf. also R. M. Grant *Augustine to Constantine*, 1971, pp.8ff and 171ff.

To the three orders of bishop, priest and deacon other minor orders were added, namely, porter, reader, exorcist, acolyte and subdeacon and all these were to be found in the medieval western Church. As they had fallen into disuse in the early sixteenth century it was not very difficult for the Anglican Reformers to abolish them. The latter, however, did not abolish the use of the word 'priest' in the vernacular. Its use by them did not imply any notion of ministerial or sacrificing priesthood (in the medieval Catholic sense), but rather reflected respect for tradition and a desire to use a word that would distinguish the second order of minister from the third and would not have the implications of a presbyterian system of church government. If asked to translate 'priest' into Latin they replied 'presbyter', thereby revealing that they knew of no priesthood of the ministry. With hindsight we may now regret this retention of the word 'priest' since it continues to be used to justify a view of the minister as possessing a priesthood not enjoyed by the laity.[1]

Though the historic, threefold ministry of the Church of England has been assailed by Puritans in the sixteenth and seventeenth centuries and by Protestant Nonconformists since then, it has stood the test of time. Modern schemes of unions of churches in Asia and Africa have incorporated this ministry as an essential ingredient. Like all human institutions it is fragile and open to abuse but in this imperfect world, when it functions aright, it is still the best form of church order. What follows in this paper is an attempt to set the present rites of ordination in the Church of England in their historical context and to examine ways in which they have been and can be revised.

---

[1] Such a ministerial priesthood is argued by Jean M. R. Tillard in *What Priesthood has the Ministry ?*, Grove Booklet No. 13.

# 2. THE ORDINAL OF 1662

In this section it will be our task to describe the origin and development of the Ordinal of the Church of England. We begin with the year 1550 because it was then, following a decade of reforming activity, that the House of Lords passed a bill on 1st February authorizing the provision of a new Ordinal to replace the medieval Pontificals.[1] The drafting committee, led by Archbishop Cranmer, did its work very quickly and in March there was published, *The forme and maner of makyng and consecratyng of Archebisshoppes, Bisshoppes, Priestes and Deacons*.[2] It made no provision for the ordination of men to the minor orders. Further, it began with an important preface in which was explained the structure of the three services and the qualifications of ordinands were stated. The structure of the first two services was as follows:

| Deacon | Priest |
|---|---|
| Sermon | Sermon |
| | Introit: Psalm 40, 132 or 135 |
| | Communion Service up to the collect of the day |
| | Epistle: Acts 20.17-35 or 1 Tim. 3 |
| | Gospel: Matt. 28.18-20, John 10.1-16 or John 20.19-23 |
| | Hymn: 'Come Holy Ghost' |
| Presentation and question as to suitability | Presentation and question as to suitability |
| Brief final enquiry of people | Final enquiry of people |
| Litany with special suffrage | Litany with special suffrage |
| Special Collect | Special Collect |
| Communion Service up to the collect of the day | |
| Epistle: 1 Tim. 3.8-13 or Acts 6.2-7 | |
| Oath of Supremacy | Oath of Supremacy |
| | Exhortation to Candidates |
| Examination | Examination and prayer |
| | Silent prayer |
| | Salutation |
| | Prayer |
| Imposition of hands by bishop with special formula | Imposition of hands by bishop (joined by priests) with special formula |
| Delivery of New Testament with formula | Delivery of Bible, Chalice and Bread with formula |
| Creed | Gospel of the Day |
| | Creed |
| Completion of Service of Holy Communion with special final collect | Completion of Service of Holy Communion with special final collect |

The service for the consecration of bishops is similar in form to that for the ordaining of priests. The Gospel is John 21.15-17 or 10.1-16. Additional features include the reading of the King's mandate for the consecration, the laying of the Bible on the neck of the new bishop and the delivery of the pastoral staff.

[1] For the background see Paul F. Bradshaw, *The Anglican Ordinal* (Alcuin Club Collections, No. 53), 1971, pp.18ff. I found this book very helpful.
[2] The Text is in F. E. Brightman, *The English Rite*, 1915, Vol. II, pp.928ff.

The guiding hand behind the creation of this Ordinal is generally acknow-ledged to have been Cranmer, who likewise was the main inspiration behind the Book of Common Prayer of 1549. However, there has been some debate in scholarly circles as to the sources used by Cranmer and his colleagues in the composition of the new Ordinal. Today most scholars accept that the Archbishop had before him a draft ordination service composed by Martin Bucer, the Lutheran reformer, who came to England at Cranmer's request.[1] Bucer's draft was a single rite as follows:

Sermon
Hymn: 'Come Holy Ghost'
Introit: Psalm 40, 132 or 155
Epistle: Acts 20.17-35; 1 Tim. 3; Eph. 4.1-16 or Titus 1.5-9
Psalm 67
Gospel: Matt. 28.18-20: John 10.1-16; 20.19-23 or 21.16-17
Final Enquiry of the People
Exhortation to the candidates
Examination and Prayer
Silent Prayer
Salutation
Prayer
Imposition of the hands of ministers with blessing
Creed
Communion Service

Using this as his basis Cranmer inserted into it further material suitable to each of the rites for the ordering of the three types of ministers. The additional material came from the Roman Catholic Pontificals, the Book of Common Prayer (1549) and from Cranmer's own wealth of liturgical knowledge.

Basic to this Reformation Ordinal is the principle that services of ordination are to be based on the teaching of Holy Scripture, especially the practice of the Church of the New Testament, but yet they may include material of a traditional and symbolic nature if it does not obviously contradict the plain principles of Scripture.[2] In particular, Cranmer held the following views. First, ordination is not a sacrament but a public service of worship in which men are set apart for the work of the ministry and for which task they and the Church request of God the gift of the Holy Spirit.[3] Secondly, the essence of ordination is prayer to God accompanied by the laying on of hands (cf. Acts 6.6, 13.3, 1 Tim. 4.14, 5.22). Thirdly, there are only two

---

[1] Bucer's rite, De ordinatione legitima ministrorum ecclesiae revocanda, was printed in his Scripta Anglicana, Basel 1577, pp.238ff. It has now been made generally available in English in the recent Alcuin Club edition, E. C. Whitaker Martin Bucer and the Book of Common Prayer (Mayhew-McCrimmon, 1974).

[2] For Cranmer's general theological position see P. E. Hughes, The Theology of the English Reformers, 1965, and The Work of Thomas Cranmer, ed. G. E. Duffield, 1964.

[3] Since he held that the presbyterate had been instituted by Christ, he adapted words used by Christ in the commissioning of the apostles. In using the words of John 20.23 he was following the custom of medieval rites. However, while holding that the gift of the Holy Spirit was given in ordination Cranmer, along with Latimer and Jewel, did not believe that the presbyter possessed any special power to absolve sin. See further R. T. Beckwith, Priesthood and Sacraments, 1964, pp.30-31.

*basic* types of ministers, deacons and presbyters; bishops and archbishops are presbyters (priests) to whom is given the special task of being chief shepherds of the flock of Christ. Fourthly, the imperative formulas ('Take thou . . .') served to delineate and distinguish the nature of the office which the ordinand was taking up; they were not of the essence of ordination as some medieval writers had thought. Fifthly, the *porrectio instrumentorum* (e.g. Bible, Chalice and Staff) were not essential but merely permissible ceremonies. Sixthly, the traditional practice of deacons being ordained by the bishop, priests being ordained by the bishop assisted by other priests, and bishops being consecrated by at least three other bishops was to be followed as there was nothing inherently objectionable in it.

When the Prayer Book was revised in 1552 some minor changes were also made in the Ordinal. The latter were in a Protestant direction and owed not a little to the influence of Bishop Hooper[1]. From the title of the Ordinal the word 'Archbishops' was removed even though it was retained in the title of the rite for the episcopate. Further, all directions about vestments and the Introits were omitted. Changes occurred also in the *porrectio instrumentorum:* priests were not given the Chalice but only a Bible, and bishops were not given a pastoral staff. The revised Ordinal was henceforth bound up with the Prayer Book although it kept its own title-page.

After the tragic interlude of Mary's reign, the Ordinal was restored (with several minor alterations) by Elizabeth.[2] Despite continuing Puritan criticism it remained unchanged throughout the reigns of James I and Charles I. Finally its use and that of the whole Prayer Book was prohibited by the Long Parliament in 1642 at the same time that diocesan episcopacy was abolished.[3] During the Commonwealth and Protectorate the majority of ordinations were according to a presbyterian or congregational form. The year 1660, however, saw the restoration of Charles II to his throne and Episcopacy and the Prayer Book to the English Church. In the subsequent revision of the Book of Common Prayer during 1661-2 changes were made in the Ordinal and not a few of these were aimed at excluding puritan interpretations of the rites and of stressing the necessity of episcopal ordination. For example, the Preface was rewritten in order to demand episcopal ordination as essential, a new epistle, Eph. 4.7-13, replaced 1 Tim. 3 (to avoid the equation of bishop and presbyter) in the rite for priests, the imperative formulae for the priesthood and episcopate were expanded in order to show that priests and bishops were two different orders, not different degrees of the one order, and, in the Litany, prayer was made for 'bishops, priests and deacons' not for 'bishops, pastors and ministers'.[4]

---

1  For details see C. W. Dugmore, 'The First Ten Years' in *The English Prayer Book, 1549-1662*, (S.P.C.K., 1963), pp.6-30.

2  Lest there be any doubts about the legality of the Ordinal ,Article 36 of the *Articles of Religion* (1562) confirmed that the 'Book of Consecration of Archbishops and Bishops and Ordering of Priests and Deacons lately set forth in the time of Edward the Sixth and confirmed by authority of Parliament' was still the legal form of ordination.

3  For Puritan criticism of the Ordinal see Bradshaw, *op. cit.,* pp.55ff.

4  Cf. W. K. Firminger, *The Alterations in the Ordinal of 1662: Why were they made?*, Church Historical Society, XXXI, 1898.

The Act of Uniformity of 1662 required all ministers of the Church of England to be episcopally ordained and to state their belief that the revised Book of Common Prayer contained nothing contrary to the Word of God. Those who could not or would not meet these conditions were expelled from their parishes, colleges or schools and forced into the position of being Protestant Nonconformists. Today, while Anglican evangelicals honour the Puritans for their concern for the purity of the Church, they are able to view the Ordinals of 1552 and 1662 rather more objectively than their zealous forebears, and they can recognise that the Ordinal of 1662, even with the changes introduced by the High Churchmen in Convocation in 1661, remains substantially the same rite as was created by the English Reformers in 1550 and 1552.

The new rite for the priesthood was as follows:

1. Introduction
    a.  Service of Morning Prayer
    b.  Sermon
    c.  Presentation by the Archdeacon, Bishop's Address and the final *Si Quis*
    d.  Commendation of the Candidates to the Congregation
    e.  Litany with special suffrage

2. Holy Communion and Ordination
    a.  Introduction to service of Holy Communion as far as collect of day
    b.  Collect
    c.  Epistle: Eph. 4.7-14
    d.  Gospel: Matt. 9.36-8 or John 10.1-16
    e.  Exhortation by the Bishop on the nature of the ministry
    f.  Examination of the Candidates in eight questions
    g.  Bishop's prayer of blessing
    h.  Silent Prayer
    i.  Hymn: 'Veni Creator Spiritus'
    j.  Thanksgiving and Prayer
    k.  Imposition of hands with the first formula 'Receive the Holy Ghost . . .'
    l.  Delivery of the Bible with the second formula 'Take thou authority . . .'
    m.  Remainder of Communion Service from Nicene Creed to the *Gloria*

3. Conclusion
    a.  Prayer for new priests
    b.  The Collect, 'Prevent us . . .'
    c.  The Benediction.

In the rite for bishops the Epistle is 1 Tim 3.1-16 and the two alternatives for the Gospel are John 21.15-17 and John 20.19-23. The consecration of the Bishop follows the Creed and the only instrument of office given to him is a Bible. Deacons are ordained after the Epistle (1 Tim. 3.8-13 or Acts 6.2-7); the Gospel in their rite is Luke 12.35-38 and the only instrument of office is a New Testament.

# 3. REVISION OF THE ORDINAL 1662-1928

From 1662 to 1689 various attempts were made to comprehend within the ministry of the Established Church such dissenting ministers as were desirous of entering it. In discussions surrounding these moves, which inevitably included the question of ordination and the Ordinal, Richard Baxter, the indefatigable negotiator, was prominent, but they came to nothing. Later suggestions for revision came within the Church of England alone. One recurring criticism was the formula of ordination beginning 'Receive the Holy Ghost . . .' which refers to the forgiving and retaining of sins. (John 20.23).

In 1792 the Episcopal Church in America provided as an alternative this formula:

> 'Take thou authority to execute the office of a priest in the Church of God, now committed unto thee by the imposition of hands. And be thou a faithful dispenser of the Word of God and of His Holy Sacraments. In the name of the Father and of the Son and of the Holy Ghost.'

It is interesting to note that though John Wesley came to believe that there was no essential difference between the presbyter-priest and the bishop he nevertheless retained the formula, 'Receive the Holy Ghost', while omitting the later words 'whose sins thou dost forgive . . .', in his service for the ordaining of ministers.[1]

During the nineteenth century whem members of the Oxford Movement began to see their own views of ministerial priesthood reflected in the contents of the Ordinal, especially in the imperative formula which is based on John 20.23, some Low Churchmen, led by the persistent Lord Ebury, made determined attempts to reform both the Prayer Book and Ordinal. For example, they wished to change the Preface of the Ordinal in order to remove the strong doctrine of episcopal ordination and instead of an imperative formula of ordination (which could be interpreted in the sense that the Bishop was passing on the Holy Spirit) they suggested a prayer to God requesting the gift of the Spirit for the ordinands.[2]

In Ireland, after the disestablishment of the Church by Gladstone, there was intense discussion of the Ordinal in the 1870's but in the revised Prayer Book of 1878 no change was made in the actual words of ordination. One reason was the fear that ordination in Ireland would not be acceptable in England unless the imperative formulae were used. However, a paragraph concerning the Ordinal was inserted in the Preface to the whole Prayer Book and this denied that any form of ministerial presthood was intended by the ancient imperative formula.[3]

---

[1] For Wesley's views see A. B. Lawson, *John Wesley and the Christian Ministry*, 1963.

[2] A. E. Peaston, *The Prayer Book Revisions of the Victorian Evangelicals*, 1963, pp.25-6. It is interesting to observe that Anglo-Catholics now argue that the best form of ordination is prayer accompanied by the laying on of hands since this is claimed as the primitive practice of the Church.

[3] *Ibid.* p.39.

Moving into the twentieth century we find that evangelicals opposed the moves in the Convocation between 1908 and 1919 to change the wording of the question concerning Scripture which is asked of deacons.[1] For several decades the impact of the higher criticism of the Bible had been felt in the Church and this proposal resulted from this. The opposition was a success and thus the Ordinal which was submitted to Parliament with the rest of the Book of Common Prayer in 1927 contained no major changes. However, had the House of Bishops had its way the Ordinal would have contained a rite for the ordaining of deaconesses. The rite was adopted by the Upper Houses of the Convocations of Canterbury and York in 1924 and its content was as follows:

1. Presentation and Question as to suitability
2. Final Enquiry of the People
3. Silent Prayer
4. Collect
5. Epistle: 1 Cor. 12.4-11
6. Examination
7. Imposition of the hands of the bishop and formula 'Take thou authority . . .'
8. Delivery of the New Testament with formula 'Be diligent to study . . .'
9. Gospel: Luke 10.38-42 or Matt. 28.1-10
10. Holy Communion
11. Special Collect
12. Prayer 'Prevent us . . .'
13. Blessing

Since it was added to the Prayer Book without the agreement of the Houses of clergy and laity it was removed from the book.[2]

---

[1] Dr. Henry Wace led this opposition: see, for example, *Chronicle of Convocation* (1912), pp.586-7.

[2] Bradshaw, *op. cit.*, p.165 has a helpful chart showing the relationship of the draft services produced by the two Convocations as well as the final rite.

## 4. THE ORDINAL AND REUNION: TWO EXAMPLES

In this section we shall examine briefly two ordinals which have been produced, at least in part, by Anglicans during the last twenty years and as part of schemes of reunion. The first is the Ordinal of the Church of South India, first published in 1958 and now part of *The Book of Common Worship of the Church of South India* (1963). Since this Church was formed by the unification of Anglican, Methodist, Presbyterian and Congregationalist elements, those who composed the Ordinal were perhaps wise to prepare a completely new rite appropriate for a new Church.[1] To this end efforts were made to incorporate material from the ordination rites of the Church of the third, fourth and fifth centuries. Also an attempt was made to follow what was believed to be a Biblical pattern. In the preface to the Ordinal it is stated that in the earliest ordination on record that described in Acts 6.1-6, there are three parts: election by the people, prayer to God and the laying on of apostolic hands. On this basis the services for the ordination of deacons, presbyters and bishops have three parts. In the words of the Preface they are:

1. The presentation of the candidates to the presiding Bishop, this being the last step in the process of choice of them by the Church.
2. Prayer for those about to be ordained or consecrated that they may receive the gift of the Holy Spirit for their ministry.
3. The laying on of hands of at least three Bishops (in an episcopal consecration), of the Bishops and Presbyters (in an ordination of Presbyters), or of the Bishop (in an ordination of Deacons).

Various ceremonies (e.g. the delivery of instruments of office—Bible and Pastoral Staff) and an examination of the candidates is added to the three basic parts. However, the Preface states that these are not essential to ordination.

The structure of all three services is therefore basically the same since each one contains the Presentation, the Ministry of the Word, the Examination and the Ordination, all set in the context of a service of Holy Communion. We may illustrate this by setting out the contents of the rite for the ordination of presbyters.

1. The Preparation from the Service of Holy Communion
2. The Presentation of the Candidates
   a. Candidates presented to Bishop by a duly appointed person
   b. Bishop declares his intention to ordain them
   c. Congregation affirms that the candidates are worthy to be ordained
3. The Ministry of the Word
   a. The ancient greeting—The Lord be with you
   b. Special collect for those to be ordained
   c. Old Testament reading. Ezekiel 33.1-9
   d. Psalm 99 or a Hymn
   e. Epistle: 1 Peter 5.1-11
   f. Gospel: John 10.1-16
   g. Sermon
   h. Nicene Creed
   i. Hymn

[1] See further E. C. Ratcliff, 'The Ordinal of the Church of South India', *Theology*, LXIII, 1960, pp.7ff. and T. S. Garrett, 'The Ordinal of the Church of South India', *Scottish Journal of Theology*, XII, 1959, pp.400ff.

4. The Examination
   a. Introduction by the Bishop
   b. Eleven questions put by Bishop to ordinands relating to their calling by God, motivation in seeking ordination, acceptance of the authority of Scriptures and creeds, diligence in study of Scriptures, tesitfying to others of God's grace, faithfulness in preaching and pastoral ministry, prayerful and disciplined life and submission to authority
   c. Ordinands reply
   d. Prayer for grace that they fulfil what they have promised
5. The Ordination
   a. Silent Prayer
   b. Hymn 'Veni Creator Spiritus'
   c. Ordination Prayer said by Bishop
      In three parts
            (i) Praise and Thanks to God
           (ii) Request to God for the gift of Holy Spirit for ordinands
          (iii) Further petitions for grace for ordinands
      During (ii) the Bishop, joined by the Presbyters, lays his hands on each of the ord inands, repeating the central part of the prayer
   d. Imp erative formula with the delivery of the Bible
   e. The giving of the right hand of fellowship
   f. The singing of the doxology
6. Completion of the service of Holy Communion.
      Special petitions for the new presbyters are included

In agreement with Cranmer's Ordinal these rites of the Church of South India presuppose that bishops and presbyters are not essentially different· This is symbolically represented in the rubric allowing presbyters to join with bishops in the consecration of a new bishop. Other admirable features are the thoroughness of the questions in the Examination and the authority to minister in Christ's name being given in, and associated with, the prayer for the gift of the spirit and the laying on of hands. The giving of the right hand of fellowship has a good Biblical basis (Galatians 2.9) as well as a good Nonconformist pedigree. The delivery of a Bible to deacons makes sense in terms of what they actually read in churches and the delivery to the Bishop of a staff is a harmless, symbolic act, emphasising that he is a chief shepherd.

Criticisms may of course be made. The lack of variety between the there rites is a weakness of the Ordinal. So also is the formula by which the congregation assents to the ordination. The people say 'We trust they are worthy'. A more fitting way could have been devised which did not leave open the possibility that onlookers could think that the ordinands possessed any human qualities which made them worthy to be Christ's ministers. Finally, it may be remarked that no attempt is made to justify on Biblical grounds the setting of an ordination within the context of a service of Holy Communion. The fact is merely taken for granted.

\*    \*    \*    \*

The second Ordinal is that produced by the Anglican-Methodist Unity Commission and printed in *Anglican-Methodist Unity: Part I. The Ordinal* (1968).[1] In content this Ordinal owes much more to the Ordinal of the Church of South India than to either the Anglican Ordinal of 1662 or the Methodist Ordinal. The reason for this is that the late Professor E. C. Ratcliff, who drafted the greater part of the Anglican-Methodist Ordinal, was also influential in the drafting of the South India Ordinal. The Preface to 'the Form and Manner of Ordaining Ministers in the Church of God according to the Order of the Church of England and the Methodist Church in Great Britain' follows the principles laid down in the Preface to the C.S.I. Ordinal by stating the following:

> The form of ordination in each case (Deacon, Priest, Bishop) follows the scriptural pattern of acceptance by the people and prayer with the laying on of hands. In each, therefore, will be found the presentation of candidates to the presiding Bishop, which is the last step in the process of choice by the Church, and prayer for the gift of the Spirit which is needed for the work of the Order to which the person is being ordained, together with the laying on of hands by the presiding Bishop...

This all means that each of the three services has the following elements: The Ministry of the Word, the Presentation of the Candidates, the Examination, the Supplication, the Ordination, the Delivery of the Bible and the Holy Communion.

The contents of the rite for 'The Ordination of Presbyters also called Priests' are as follows:

1. The beginning of the Communion Service
   a. Hymn
   b. Collect
   c. Epistle: Romans 12.1-12
   d. Gospel: John 20.19-29
   e. Sermon
   f. Nicene Creed
2. The Presentation
   a. Ordinands presented to the Bishop by a duly appointed person
   b. Names of Ordinands read out
   c. Bishop announces his intention to ordain them
   d. Congregation declares its assent to the ordination
   e. Short homily (optional)
3. The Examination
   a. Bishop asks seven questions relating to the calling of God, acceptance of the Scriptures, doctrines of the Faith, discipline of the Church, diligence in prayer and study, faithfulness in ministry, and the making of Christ known to men.
   b. Ordinands reply
   c. Bishop prays that they may be given grace to perform what they have promised.

---

[1] I found Roger T. Beckwith's arguments helpful: 'The Proposed Anglican-Methodist Ordinal', *The Churchman*, Vol. 81, No. 3, Autumn 1967.

4. The Supplication
    a.   Bishop calls the congregation to silent prayer
    b.   The hymn 'Veni Creator Spiritus' is said or sung

5. The Ordination
    a.   Ordination prayer said by the Bishop. It has three parts, an address with thanksgiving, the petition for the Holy Spirit, and prayer for grace in relation to some particular duties of the presbyterate.
    b.   The laying on of hands by the Bishop assisted by presbyters. This takes place during the central petition and is repeated over each candidate

6. The Delivery of the Bible
    a.   Bible given to each presbyter with the words 'Take this Book, a token of the authority which you have received from God . . .'

7. The Completion of the Communion Service
    a.   The new presbyters join with other presbyters and with the Bishop in reciting the Thanksgiving
    b.   A special prayer for the new presbyters is said after Communion

Though this rite, as well as those for deacons and bishops, is modelled on the C.S.I. rite, it and they do incorporate some changes. The presentation of the candidates follows rather than precedes the ministry of the Word and no pastoral staff is given to the new Bishop. Some changes weaken the Ordinal: for example, the opening collect is inferior, the examination of the candidates is less demanding, the readings from Scripture are less appropriate, presbyters do not join with bishops in consecrating a bishop, and a vague type of concelebration is introduced in the Communion Service. One change, however, is an improvement: the homily in the presentation of the candidates is longer but unfortunately it is optional.

# 5. THE NEW ROMAN ORDINAL

In the Introduction to the Commentary on the Anglican-Methodist Ordinal it is stated that the drafting committee was kept informed about the revision of the Roman Catholic rites of ordination. Although the latter seem to have had no obvious influence on the final product the same cannot be said of the experimental Ordinal of the Episcopal Church, U.S.A. Furthermore, the possibility cannot be ruled out that the Liturgical Commission of the Church of England will not be influenced by the Roman rites. Therefore, before we look at the American Ordinal and comment on the revision of the Ordinal of 1662, it will be helpful briefly to notice the contents of the Roman rites. These were printed for private circulation by the Vatican Press in 1968 under the title *De Ordinatione Diaconi, Presbyteri et Episcopi.* Copies of this are rare and cannot be bought from booksellers. An English translation of part of this has been prepared by the International Committee for English in the Liturgy under the title, *The Rite of Ordination of Deacons and Priests,* but again this is only for private circulation in seminaries and cathedrals.[1] The structure of the rites for the ordaining of deacons and priests are as follows:

| Deacons | Priests |
|---|---|
| The Liturgy of the Word up to the Gospel of the day | The Liturgy of the Word up to the Gospel of the day |
| The Presentation of the Candidates | The Presentation of the Candidates |
| The Election and Acceptance by the Congregation | The Election and Acceptance by the Congregation |
| The Bishop's Address | The Bishop's Address |
| Vow of celibacy | — |
| The Examination in five questions | The Examination in five questions |
| Supplication: Litany of the Saints | Supplication: Litany of the Saints |
| The laying on of hands in silence (done by the Bishop alone) | The laying on of hands in silence (done by Bishop joined by priests) |
| The Prayer of Consecration said by the Bishop | The Prayer of Consecration said by the Bishop |
| The Investiture in stole and dalmatic | The Investiture in stole and chasuble |
| | The Anointing of the palms of the hands of each new priest by the Bishop (Choir sings 'Veni Creator Spiritus') |
| Delivery of the Book of Gospels with a formula | Delivery of the Chalice and Paten with a formula |
| The Kiss of Peace | The Kiss of Peace |
| The Liturgy of the Eucharist, with new deacons assisting | The Liturgy of the Eucharist, with the new presbyters concelebrating |

Only a few comments are necessary. First, the reason why the vow of celibacy appears in the service for the ordaining of deacons is because the sub-diaconate has now been formally abolished and so the vow is no longer taken as formerly when the office of sub-deacon was given. Secondly, the laying on of hands in silence is an ancient practice in the Western Church and can be traced back to the fifth century. Thirdly, these new rites still preserve two strong Roman doctrines, the priesthood of the ministry and the episcopate as being the primary ministry within the Church.

---

[1] I am grateful to Bishop Gray of Liverpool and the Rev. John Short of Upholland College and Seminary for loaning me copies of the I.C.E.L. text and that used in the Metropolitan Cathedral, Liverpool. I understand that the R.C. hierarchy in England has commissioned a new translation of the rites since it prefers traditional words such as 'priest' to the literal translation of the I.C.E.L. which has 'presbyter'.

## 6. THE EXPERIMENTAL RITES OF THE EPISCOPAL CHURCH, U.S.A.

A new Ordinal has been produced by the Standing Liturgical Commission of the Episcopal Church, U.S.A., as part of the general programme of Prayer Book Revision. It was published with an Introduction as *The Ordination of Bishops, Priests and Deacons; Prayer Book Studies, 20.* (1970), was approved by the General Convention in 1970, and is now in trial use. In general form the rites follow the structure of the C.S.I. and Anglican/Methodist Ordinals but they show the influence of both the new Roman rites and known ordination rites of the fourth and fifth centuries. The printed order of the rites reflects the latter influence and the reasons given in the Introduction are 'to indicate the centrality of the episcopate' and to follow the arrangement of the liturgical books of the Early Church. The contents of the service for the ordaining of a priest (in the U.S.A. ordinations are usually of one man only in his parish church) are as follows:

1. Introduction to the Communion Service
   a. A Psalm, Hymn or Anthem
   b. Introductory sentences of praise to God
   c. Collect for purity

2. The Presentation
   a. A priest and lay-person present the candidate
   b. Bishop asks ordinand if he will be loyal to the doctrine, discipline and worship of the Church and obey his Bishop
   c. Ordinand replies
   d. Bishop states his intention to ordain and asks if there are any objections
   e. Congregation assents to the ordination
   f. Bishop calls the congregation to prayer—Litany, Collect for the day and/or a special collect

3. The Ministry of the Word
   a. Old Testament Lesson: Isaiah 6.1-8 or Numbers 11.16-17, 24-5 (read by layperson)
   b. Psalm 43 or 132.8-19
   c. Epistle: 1 Peter 5.1-4 or Eph. 4.7, 11-16 or Philippians 4.4-9 (read by layperson)
   d. Gospel: Matt. 9.35-38 or John 10.11-18 or John 6.35-8 (read by a deacon or priest)
   e. Sermon
   f. The Creed

4. The Examination
   a. Brief Homily
   b. Bishop asks five questions of the ordinand which relate to his calling, commitment, faithfulness in prayer and study, service of Christ and holiness of life
   c. Ordinand replies
   d. Bishop prays God to give the ordinand grace to perform what he had promised

5. The Ordination of the Priest

    a.    Ordinand kneels in front of the bishop; priests stand to the right and left of the bishop

    b.    Hymn: 'Veni Creator Spiritus' or 'Veni Sancte Spiritus'

    c.    Silent Prayer

    d.    Bishop prays the ordination prayer, first thanksgiving, secondly petition for the gift of the Holy Spirit, thirdly, petition that he may glorify God in the ministry

    e.    During the second part of the prayer the Bishop joined by the priests, lays hands on the ordinand.

    f.    The Congregation assents in the word 'Amen'

    g.    The new priest is suitably vested

    h.    The Bishop gives the priest a Bible with the formula 'Receive this Bible as a sign of the authority given you . . .'

6. The Peace

    a.    The Bishop and other clergy greet the new priest

    b.    The new priest gives the peace to the congregation

    c.    The congregation responds

7. The Completion of the Eucharist

The new priest joins in the celebration and at the end of the service gives the blessing to the congregation.

The rubrics presuppose that the ordinand will be vested in a stole but do not require this. Presentation of chalice and paten is optional. Concerning concelebration the rubric reads:

*'the new Priest and other Priests shall stand at the Altar with the Bishop as associates and fellow-ministers, and shall communicate with him. After the Lord's Prayer, the new Priest shall, and other Priests may, join the Bishop in breaking the bread.'*

To say the least, this rubric is vague as to what exactly is concelebration.

These rites are well planned and contain several attractive features. A new Litany is provided; the participation of lay people is required; optional Scripture readings are given and intercession is emphasised. Doctrinally, however, they leave much to be desired. Ministerial priesthood, apostolic succession, and a sacramental view of ordination are all implied in the words of the services and suggested in the words of the Introduction. One regrettable clause in the ordination prayer for a bishop requests that 'he may exercise without reproach the high priesthood to which You have called him'. Ironically an optional reading in the same service is Hebrews 5.1-10 which teaches that Christ alone possesses the high priesthood. It is of course well known that the American Episcopal Church is high church in tradition, and some might suspect that it is desirous of making its liturgy approximate as far as possible to that of the Church of Rome.

## 7. FUTURE REVISION OF THE ORDINAL OF 1662

One of the current tasks of the Liturgical Commission of the Church of England is to produce a new Ordinal for inclusion in a new Prayer Book. A primary question to which the Commission will presumably have to apply itself will be this. Should the Ordinal of 1662 be modernised and improved, or should a new type of Ordinal, based on the tradition set by the Church of South India and the Anglican-Methodist Commission, be produced? In view of this we shall look at both alternatives and offer some suggestions for the improvement of each one. A second question, to which the Commission will also pay some attention, will be this: should a rite for the ordaining of deaconesses be included in the Ordinal and if so, which one? We shall also offer a comment concerning this problem. First, then, we shall make suggestions for the improvement of the Anglican-Methodist Ordinal.[1]

As they now stand the three rites are very similar and some variety needs to be introduced. For example, the rite for the ordaining of deacons could be simplified (or the rite for the ordaining of priests enriched) in order to stress the greater importance in the Church of the presbyterate. Secondly, a way needs to be found to maintain the proximity of the ordination prayer and the laying on of hands which does not interrupt the flow of the prayer and which does not necessitate the repetition of the central petition. One way would be to follow the Roman rite and lay hands on each ordinand in silence. Another would be to shorten the ordination prayer and repeat it over each ordinand. Thirdly, the questions in the Examination need both strengthening and varying for each rite. In these days of apostasy and challenge, the Church cannot afford to weaken the ordination promises of her ministers[2]. Fourthly, alternative Scripture readings should be introduced in all services and the use of the same Epistle for the rites of the diaconate and presbyterate should be abandoned. The Bible is a sufficiently rich book for a variety of suitable readings to be made available! Fifthly, the exhortation to those to be ordained priest (the homily in the Presentation) needs to be made compulsory and to be extended by the addition of further suitable material. This part of the Presentation serves to emphasise the high calling of God to which the presbyter is called. Sixthly, all references (however vague) to ministerial priesthood, to a sacramental view of ordination and to apostolic succession which appear in the Preface and in the ordination prayers for presbyters and bishops should be removed

---

[1] My suggestions are based on the expectation that the threefold ministry will continue in England in the next decade much as it has in the past decade. However, personally speaking, I would welcome the cessation of the practice of ordaining men first to the diaconate and a year later to the presbyterate. I feel that the diaconate should be a separate ministry of service and compassion to which men and women are ordained for life. Candidates for the ministry of Word and Sacrament (be it a full or part-time ministry) should be ordained to the presbyterate after a suitable period of training and testing. On the question of the ordination of women to the presbyterate I have an open mind. (The above was written before the recent report recommending the abolition of the diaconate was published).

[2] The two questions, for example, on Scripture and the doctrines of the Faith are too weak. The C.S.I. rite is decidedly superior; it specifically refers to Scripture as 'the supreme and decisive standard of faith' and, in regard to doctrine, actually specifies the Creeds.

since they have no Biblical warrant.[1] Seventhly, there needs to be a greater emphasis on intercession: silent prayer and the *Veni Creator Spiritus* are fine but to them (as in the American rites) could be added a modernised form of the Litany, or at least something similar. Eighthly, the participation of lay-people in the services should be obligatory: they can present the candidates, read the lessons and lead the intercessions. Ninthly, the *porrectio instrumentorum* could be as follows: Bible to Deacons, Bible and Chalice to Priests, Bible and Staff to Bishops. Tenthly, the rubrics (e.g. concerning newly ordained deacons assisting in the distribution at the Communion and concelebration by newly ordained presbyters) should be improved and to them could be added specific instructions (with options built into them) concerning the proper dress of the ordinand both before and after the ordination.[2] Finally, the rite for the ordaining of deacons should be used for the ordaining of deaconesses.

Turning now to the Ordinal of 1662 we note that it contains much more variety than the newer Ordinals. The usage of the Church of England has been to ordain deacons after the Epistle, priests after the Gospel and bishops after the Creed. This variety is a feature which ought to be preserved. Indeed, any revision of the 1662 Services must of necessity be conservative if the end product is to be recognised as a revision of 1662! So, taking for granted that there will be a modernisation of the language of the Ordinal, we shall first make some general comments about the Preface and Services and secondly make specific comments about each of the three rites.

The first sentence of the Preface will have to be reworded so as not to give the impression that the threefold ministry was universal in the apostolic age. The third sentence calls in question the validity of the ordinations within such churches as the Church of Scotland and the Lutheran Churches of Europe. For the sake of charity, ecumenism and Biblical theology it should be changed. Finally the qualifications of a minister, as described in the third paragraph, will need further revision since the qualifications for entry into the presbyterate are constantly under review.

Concerning the general structure of the rites, Morning Prayer should be made optional as it is usually said by the ordinands in their retreat house and as it lengthens the services unduly. The sermon would then follow the reading of Scripture. Ordination should be (either as in the C.S.I. rite or the Roman rite) by prayer and the laying on of hands[3]. The imperative formula

---

[1] Section 4 of the Preface speaks of the ministry of deacons, priests and bishops as a *special form* (italics mine) of the royal priesthood which the whole Church has received from Christ. This idea of a special form is repeated in the ordination prayer said by the Bishop in the rite for ordaining presbyters; he prays 'that within the royal priesthood of thy People they may faithfully fulfil their priestly ministry'. A view of apostolic succession comes through in the ordination prayer for a bishop: the presiding bishop prays God to 'endue him . . . as thou didst endue thine apostles, with the fullness of thy grace'.

[2] For example, rules should be so worded as not to compel ordinands to wear a stole. Pressure is still sometimes brought to bear on this point. There is of course no basis for it in rubrics or Canon Law.

[3] The prayers of ordination should specifically request that the gift of the Holy Spirit appropriate to the specified order of ministry may be given by God to the ordinand(s).

'Receive the Holy Ghost . . .', though based on John 20.22-23, is a uniquely Dominical statement not repeatable by bishops. An imperative formula (as in C.S.I. and Anglican/Methodist rites) may, however, be used with the *porrectio instrumentorum*. Participation by laity as suggested above needs to be made obligatory. Concerning the rubrics the following could be stated:

i The singing of hymns be allowed
ii The place of ordinations be either in the cathedral or in suitable parish churches
iii The reading of the Epistle, the prayers of intercession and the presentation of the candidates be by lay-people
iv No clergy dress to be ebforced which is not required by Canon Law.

Revision of the rite for the diaconate should proceed on the principle that the orders of deacons and deaconesses will be fused. More specifically the sermon could follow the Epistle and be based on that portion of Scripture, so highlighting the nature and duties of the diaconate. The Examination, which would then follow the Sermon ,would have to be reworded to take account of the modern duties of deacons and the possibility of the permanent diaconate. Any revision here should not be allowed to tone down the rigour of the questions. Instead of presenting the deacon with a New Testament it is more fitting to give him a Bible (since he reads the Old Testament in Church) and a suitable imperative formula to be said by the Bishop. An optional Gospel (e.g. Mark 10.35-45) could be introduced alongside Luke 12.35ff. Finally, there is no reason why deacons should not join with the Bishop in laying their hands on the ordinands. This would be a sign of their welcoming him (them) into the order of deacons and will be very meaningful if there is a permanent diaconate.

In the rite for the presbyterate, the Sermon could come between the Gospel and the Bishop's Address, or, if the Bishop's Address be suitably lengthened, this could be regarded as the Sermon. Following the ordination prayer and the laying on of hands a Bible, together with a Chalice and Paten could be given. This would symbolise that the Church has now given the newly ordained presbyters the right to preach the Word and preside at the Holy Communion. If there is no hint of ministerial priesthood in the rest of the service then no ministerial priesthood could be read into the delivery of the chalice. The words 'laying aside worldly cares and studies', part of the Bishop's Address, may need to be modified not only because of the growth of the auxiliary pastoral ministry but also because of what in fact many clergy actually do today.

Finally, in the rite for the making of bishops and archbishops, the *porrectio instrumentorum* could be the Bible and the Pastoral Staff. Here the symbolism would be that the Church has set a presbyter aside to act as a chief shepherd of the flock of Christ.

Living in a technological world we have a greater need of visible symbolism in our religion than did our forefathers. Hence the suggestions made concerning the variety in the *porrectio instrumentorum*.[1] Attractive symbolism and sound doctrine can exist harmoniously together.

1 On the question of symbolism see E. Bevan, *Symbolism and Belief*, 1963; F. W. Dillistone, *Traditional Symbols and the Contemporary World*, 1973 and R. Firth, *Symbols: Public and Private*, 1973.

# APPENDIX

The Order of Service for the ordination in Liverpool Cathedral on 30 June, 1974 was entitled: 'THE SERVICE OF HOLY COMMUNION with the Form and Manner of Making of Deacons and Ordering of Priests'. The contents were a combination of Series 3 Holy Communion and the Ordinal of 1662.

a. Introduction
- a. Litany
- b. The Greeting
- c. The Collect for purity
- d. Gloria in Excelsis (Choir)
- e. Two further Collects (of the day and from Ordinal)

b. Ministry of the Word
- a. Psalm 146 (Choir)
- b. Epistle: 2 Cor. 5.14-20
- c. Hymn: 'Praise we now the Word of grace'
- d. Gospel: Luke 4.16-21
- e. Sermon

c. Ordination
- a. Anthem 'Alleluia' (Choir)
- b. Presentation of Candidates
- c. Examination of Deacons
- d. Ordination of Deacons (by laying on of hands and with the two imperative formulae)
- e. Hymn: 'A charge to keep I have'
- f. Examination of Priests
- g. Hymn: 'Come Holy Ghost' (Choir)
- h. Ordination of priests (by laying on of hands and with the two imperative formulae)
- i. Prayers of intercession (taken from Series 3)

d. Ministry of the Sacrament

continuation of Series 3 with the preparation, the greeting, the taking of bread and wine etc.

It is obvious that the instructions given in the Ordinal concerning how the services for ordaining deacons and priests are to be united have not been followed. Of more importance is the fact that so much was left out of the Ordinal: for example, the readings from Scripture, which anchor the ministry in a Biblical foundation, the Bishop's Address to those to be ordained priest, and the actual prayers of ordination. The omission of the latter, especially that for the priesthood, is extremely serious if (according to Catholic theory) the essence of ordination be prayer to God (distinctly requesting grace for a specific order of ministry) and the laying on of hands. Apart from omissions from the Ordinal, the Creed was also omitted from the service of Holy Communion.

## GROVE BOOKLETS ON MINISTRY AND WORSHIP

The titles in the series thus far are listed, along with other Grove Books publications, on the outside back-cover. They should all be available immediately or by order from religious booksellers. They can also be obtained by sending cash with order (preferably with a 9" x 6" stamped addressed envelope for orders worth less than £1) to Grove Books.

**Standing Orders:** Grove Books will post to reach customers on the day of publication each Grove Booklet in the series, post free. Invoices will be sent after 6 titles have been sent.

Order from Grove Books on this slip below.

— — — — — — — — — — — — — — —

To GROVE BOOKS, BRAMCOTE, NOTTS.

Please send ............... copies of each Grove Booklet, beginning with number ..............., to my standing order. I will pay for these when I receive an invoice.

Please also send ............... copies of each Booklet on Ethics, beginning with number ................

Please send the following for which I enclose (including stamped address-ed envelope) cheque/PO/Stamps for............................

...............................................................................................................

...............................................................................................................

...............................................................................................................

NAME.........................................................................................................

ADDRESS....................................................................................................

...............................................................................................................

...............................................................................................................

(Please delete what is inapplicable. Please also write very clearly)

23